Smart Starters

Science

Motivational Exercises
to Stimulate the Brain

by Imogene Forte & Marjorie Frank

Incentive Publications
Nashville, Tennessee

Illustrated by Marta Drayton
Cover by Geoffrey Brittingham
Edited by Patience Camplair

ISBN 0-86530-641-9

1   2   3   4   5   6   7   8   9   10   08   07   06   05

PRINTED IN THE UNITED STATES OF AMERICA
www.incentivepublications.com

Table of Contents

Introduction

What is a Smart Starter?

A Smart Starter changes "extra" moments in a classroom setting into teachable moments. They are designed take short amounts of time. However, Smart Starters are NOT short on substance. The Smart Starters in this book are packed full of important skills to practice and polish or to reinforce and extend.

When are Smart Starters used?

As their name suggests, they are good for igniting learning. Instead of the slow move into a class period, lesson, or school day, a Smart Starter quick-starts the action. Each one warms up the brain with a sparkling challenge. Students also need this kind of spark at times other than the beginning of the day or class period. Use a Smart Starter any time there is a lull, or any time students need a break from a longer activity. They work effectively to stimulate thinking at the beginning, end, or middle of a class period, or any other time you can squeeze in an extra ten minutes.

Why use Smart Starters?

They're energizing! They're stimulating! They're fun! They nudge students to focus on a specific goal. They "wake-up" tired minds. They require students to make use of previously acquired knowledge and skills. Because of their short length, they give quick success and quick rewards—thus inspiring confidence and satisfaction for the learners.

How to Use This Book...

Kick-Off a New Unit

The starters are grouped by science strands. One or more of them might help to ease students into a new area of study. For instance, start off a unit on space objects with *Extraterrestrial Questions (page 45)*, or a fitness-nutrition unit with *Would You? Could You? (page 40)*. Or, use *Spinning Eggs (page 64)* to introduce students to density concepts.

Spark a Longer Lesson

Any one of these short activities can be expanded. A starter may inspire your students to develop more questions along the same lines—expanding the warm-up into a full-blown science lesson.

Review a Concept

Dust off those rusty skills with a Smart Starter. For instance: Have students been away from study of the body systems for a while? Refresh what they know about the skeletal system with *Bone Maps (page 37)*. Or, strengthen their knowledge of weather events with *Weather or Not (page 59)*. Any of these Smart Starters will help to reinforce concepts previously introduced.

Charge-Up Thinking Skills & Ignite Creativity

The Smart Starters are not only for science class. Use them any time to stimulate minds. Doing a Smart Starter will sharpen thinking processes and challenge brains. In addition, Smart Starters work well as starting points for students to create other (similar) questions and problems.

Science Everywhere You Look

This is a quick brainstorming activity to help students think about how widespread science is in their lives. Divide the topics below among groups of three or four students. You can add to the topic list to give two topics to each group.

Give the students five minutes to brainstorm examples of how science would be "found" in that location. After five minutes, trade lists with other groups so that students can benefit from the thinking of others.

backpack	circus	skating rink
kitchen	delicatessen	baseball game
mall	subway	school bus
classroom	airport	camping trip
roller coaster	elevator	movie theater

Who Studies What?

What do each of these scientists study? Find out which scientist is in which field.

1. anatomist _____

2. paleontologist _____

3. agronomist _____

4. physicist _____

5. hematologist _____

6. cryogenicist _____

7. petrologist _____

8. entomologist _____

9. cytologist _____

10. ornithologist _____

11. archaeologist _____

12. histologist _____

13. geneticist _____

14. pathologist _____

15. astrophysicist _____

16. ichthyologist _____

17. zoologist _____

18. botanist _____

Curious Questions

Can your students find the answers to these science mysteries? Divide the class into pairs or small groups. Give each group one question and ten minutes to answer it. Find time later to share the answers.

1. How does an oyster make a pearl?

2. Why is a spring tide higher than a neap tide?

3. Why does an elephant move its trunk back and forth constantly?

4. What, exactly, is a black hole?

5. When is the next time Halley's Comet will be visible from Earth?

6. What makes a diamond so hard?

7. What is the job of a vacuole?

8. Why do cats cough up hairballs?

9. What is the best way to get out of quicksand?

10. Of what material are fingernails made?

Where Would You Find It? (I)

Look at each word. Find out what the word means or names. Describe a place where this item or phenomenon would be found.

1. scapula _____

2. neuron _____

3. stalactite _____

4. white dwarf _____

5. uvula _____

6. medulla _____

7. tombolo _____

8. monsoon _____

9. Leonid storm _____

10. flagellum _____

11. quark _____

12. cirrus _____

13. fumarole _____

14. doldrums _____

15. moraine _____

16. chlorophyll _____

17. vacuole _____

18. a spit _____

Measurement Know-How

Most science investigations make use of metric measurements. Do this quick oral exercise to practice measurement conversions with students. Read these measurements aloud. Students should give the answers as speedily as possible.

1. 30 grams. How many milligrams? _____

2. 25 liters. How many milliliters?_____

3. 1,700 grams. How many kilograms?_____

4. 7 metric tons. How many kilograms? ____

5. 4.6 meters. How many centimeters? _____

6. 3 kilometers. How many millimeters? ____

7. 147 milliliters. How many liters? _____

8. 25.5 kilometers. How many meters? _____

9. 95° F. How many °C? _____

10. 10 inches. How many centimeters? _____

11. 20 kilograms. How many pounds?_____

12. 100 miles. How many kilometers? _____

13. 50 liters. How many quarts? _____

14. 10 yards. How many meters? _____

15. 1,000 ounces. How many grams? _____

16. 10 quarts. How many liters? _____

Formula Wisdom

Make a copy of this page, and cut out each box. Give one of these problems to a small group of students. Students must find the correct formula and use it to solve the problem.

1. John has a bag with 3,500 cm³ of gumdrops. Will this fit into a box that is 20 x 25 x 10 cm?

2. A turtle crawls around the perimeter of a 80 x 45 m field. If his speed is 50 meters per hour, how long will it take him to get around the field?

3. Can Charlie fit 200 cm³ of soda pop in a 20 cm tall cylindrical can with a 10 cm radius?

4. Abby is filling a new ball with air. The ball has a 16 cm diameter. Will it hold 300 cm³ of air?

5. Some kids want to paint a trapezoid-shaped design on the bottom of the swimming pool. The trapezoid has an 8 m base and a 6.5 m base. Its height is 7 m. Each can of the paint covers 25 square meters and costs $12.50. How much will it cost for the paint to do the design?

6. Can Suzie put 3 liters of energy juice into a cone-shaped container with a 30 cm height and a 20 cm diameter?

   (Note: One liter is equal to 1,000 cubic centimeters.)

More Formula Wisdom

Brush up on other formula skills with these science problems. Make a copy of this page, and cut out the boxes. Divide students into groups, giving one problem to each group. Later, students can make up other problems to trade and solve.

1. A screwdriver 22 cm in length opens a can with an edge measuring 0.5 cm. What is the mechanical advantage of the screwdriver?	4. How much energy will it take to raise a pot of 2 kg of water from 10° C to 60° C?
2. A hammer with a mechanical advantage of 15 pulls out a nail with a resistance force of 4,500 Newtons. What effort force is needed to pull the nail out of a wooden beam?	5. A hairdryer uses power from a source of 120 volts. It uses 15A (amperes) of current. What is the wattage of the hairdryer?
3. An elevator weighs 30,000 N. It is lifted 30 m in 50 seconds. How much power must the elevator's motor generate to do this job?	6. A child pushes a box of toys 35 meters across the floor. The force used is 10 Newtons. How much work is done?

Laws & Theories

Review with students the definition of a law and a theory. Note the differences between them. Then, employ science research skills to track down the explanation or details of these key laws and theories.

A **scientific law** (or principle) is a "rule" that describes the behavior of something in nature. A law (or principle) describes something that happens.

A **scientific theory** is an explanation based on many observations made during repeated experiments. A theory explains behavior. It tells why.

1. Heliocentric Theory
2. Theory of Relativity
3. Big Bang Theory
4. Germ Theory
5. Theory of Evolution
6. Plate Tectonics Theory
7. Theory of Superconductivity

8. Newton's Third Law of Motion
9. Bernoulli's Principle
10. Mendel's Laws
11. Newton's Second Law of Motion
12. Newton's Law of Gravitation
13. Pascal's Law
14. Archimedes' Principle

Big Ideas

There are some basic, underlying concepts that relate to the natural world. Write these big science concepts on the board: change, constancy, cycle, order, organization, systems, evolution, equilibrium, form & function, cause & effect, force & motion, energy & matter. Read each example below. As an oral quiz, ask students to find the science concept that matches the example.

1. Plants use carbon dioxide to help them make oxygen, which they release into the air. Other living things use oxygen and release carbon dioxide back into the air.

2. A snail has a thick, sticky, muscular foot. The foot holds on to surfaces to help the snail move.

3. When a body temperature gets too high, the body sweats to regulate the temperature back to normal so the body does not overheat.

4. Rocks are worn away by wind carrying sand.

5. The temperature of boiling water stays the same, even if the heat is increased.

6. A woman pulls her canoe paddle backwards in the water. The canoe moves forward.

7. Year after year, fall follows summer and spring follows winter.

8. A predator gets close to a rattlesnake. The rattlesnake coils and shakes its rattle.

9. Several organs in the body work together to enable digestion to take place.

10. When wood burns, heat is released and the wood is changed into a different substance.

Which Process?

Processes are skills of doing. Scientists use certain processes to learn about the natural world. Below are some major science processes. Students can work in pairs to choose a process and describe an example of how it might be used in the work of a scientist.

observing	forming models
questioning	using math
comparing	summarizing data
classifying	recording data
experimenting	interpreting data
controlling variables	inferring
hypothesizing	predicting
defining operationally	communicating results

Examples:

QUESTIONING: Will mice running a maze be able to distinguish among different colors?

COMPARING: Some joints in the body bend, others rotate, swivel, or twist.

Good News, Bad News

Are scientific advances good news or bad news? You decide.

New scientific inventions or technological gadgets and processes are amazing. They can offer great benefits to the world. Many of them also present hazards. Think about each of these scientific advances. Tell some benefits and some dangerous, unhealthy, or unpleasant consequences. Brainstorm and discuss each one.

Internet	automobiles	DVD players
computers	engine-powered lawnmowers	camera
credit cards		cellular telephones
jet engine	automatic machines in factories	escalators

Which Came First?

Brush up on science history with this quick quiz. Read the question and possible answers. Let students use their knowledge to choose the right one. When time allows, use resources to find dates for the events and check the answers.

1. Which invention or discovery came first: fire, the steam engine, the telegraph, or neon lights?

2. Which invention or discovery came first: television, photocopier, light bulb, or camera?

3. Which invention or discovery came first: geometry, electricity, or passenger elevator?

4. Which invention or discovery came first: jet engine, helicopter, rocket, or airplane?

5. Which invention or discovery came first: washing machine, maps, radium, videotape?

6. Which discovery came first: electromagnetism, blood circulation, laws of heredity, or X-rays?

7. Which is most recent: mapping of human genome, invention of laser, or launch of Hubble Space Telescope?

8. Which discovery is most recent: atoms, that germs cause disease, or the planet Pluto?

9. Which invention or discovery is most recent: jet engine, steam engine, CDs, or penicillin?

10. Which is most recent: first moon walk, launch of Sputnik, or the discovery of X-rays?

Who's Who in Science?

Match the scientists with the area of their accomplishments or discoveries. Write both columns on the board. See if students can make the matches in less than ten minutes.

Column I	Column II
1. Hippocrates	A. computer languages
2. James Watt	B. electromagnetic radiation
3. Louis Pasteur	C. Sun at center of solar system
4. Marie Curie	D. heat energy
5. Copernicus	E. smallpox vaccine
6. Albert Einstein	F. father of medicine
7. Gregor Mendel	G. gravity and motion
8. James Joule	H. relativity
9. Benjamin Franklin	I. destroying diseases
10. Edward Jenner	J. radioactivity
11. Heinrich Hertz	K. electricity
12. Isaac Newton	L. genetics
13. Grace Hopper	M. power
14. Carolus Linnaeus	N. plant classification

Where Would You Find It? (II)

Look at each word. Find out about the life science feature that each word names. Describe a place where this item could be found.

1. petiole

_____

2. cambium

_____

3. stomata

_____

4. cornea

_____

5. stirrup

_____

6. plasma

_____

7. Golgi body

_____

8. atrium

_____

9. platelets

_____

10. stigma

_____

11. scavenger

_____

12. epiglottis

_____

13. iris

_____

14. parasite

_____

15. olfactory lobe

_____

16. coccyx

_____

17. xylem

_____

18. periosteum

_____

Osmosis is Not a Disease

Take this ten-question challenge to review features and processes unique to living organisms. It will strengthen your knowledge about the basics of life.

1. Osmosis may sound like a disease, but it is not. What is it? _____

2. From where to where do particles move during diffusion? _____

3. What divides during mitosis? _____

4. During what life process does a plant go limp as water diffuses out of the cells?

   _____

5. What is being released from cells during respiration? _____

6. What seven things do all living things have in common? _____

7. What feature is found in plant cells but not in animal cells? _____

8. What gets stored in a vacuole?

   _____

9. What process is the opposite of diffusion?

   _____

10. What process names the sum total of all chemical processes and changes occurring in an organism?

    _____

What Good Are Roots?

What good are they? Ask this question about each of these plant structures. Answer by telling the purpose or function of each structure.

1. What good are roots?

2. What good is xylem?

3. What good is a leaf's blade?

4. What good is a leaf's epidermis?

5. What good is cambium?

6. What good are stems?

7. What good is a petiole?

8. What good are rhizomes?

9. What good is a cone on an evergreen tree?

10. What good is a stoma?

11. What good is a taproot?

It's Not True!

Each of these statements about a plant process is not true. Listen to each statement and change a word or phrase to make the false statement true.

1. The substance in green plant cells that captures sunlight is sugar.

2. Oxygen and carbon dioxide pass in and out of a plant through the veins in its leaves.

3. The opposite process of photosynthesis is germination.

4. Carbon dioxide is produced during photosynthesis.

5. Oxygen is a byproduct of respiration.

6. Sugar is produced in a plant during transpiration.

7. A plant grows toward the sunlight. This is called geotropism.

8. Water is one of the products of photosynthesis.

Celery With Stripes

Take a closer look at one plant process by turning green celery into striped celery. Prepare the celery one day and discuss the results of the experiment the next day. (You can also do this with white flowers, such as daisies.)

1. Fill two glasses with water.

2. Put red food coloring into one glass and blue food coloring into the other.

3. Choose two stalks of celery with leaves. Cut a slice off the end of each stalk.

4. Place the cut end of each stalk into each of the glasses.

5. Examine the celery closely the next day.

6. Slice the celery crosswise to see the inside.

7. Describe what you see, and discuss how the celery might have become striped.

What's Happening?

The water travels up the stalk to the leaves or petals through tiny tubes called xylem, carrying the color with it. The upward movement of the water is called capillary action.

What's the Connection?

Ecology studies relationships between living things and their environments. Each example describes a relationship. Find the word or phrase that describes the relationship.

1. A spider traps a fly in his web.

2. Ants eat a dead worm.

3. A tick feeds on a dog.

4. An orchid lives on a tree branch without doing any harm to the tree.

5. Weeds choke out the young plants in a garden.

6. A fungus grows on a dead log, helping it to rot.

7. A small bird gets its food from between the teeth of a crocodile. The crocodile gets his teeth cleaned.

8. A mouse feeds on acorns. A snake eats the mouse. An owl eats the snake.

9. Camels, cacti, lizards, snakes, and sagebrush all live together in a section of desert.

10. Green plants make their own food and are eaten by rabbits.

Use these words:

scavenger

consumers

commensalism

dominant species

predator—prey

mutualism

decomposer

community

parasitism

food chain

Recipes for Trouble

These items are some of the troubles in the environment. Each problem has "ingredients" that contribute to it.

Name or describe a key ingredient that is part of the "recipe" for each of these troublesome conditions in the environment. Explain how the ingredient contributes to the problem.

1. acid rain _____

2. depletion of the ozone layer _____

3. greenhouse gasses _____

4. smog _____

5. thermal pollution in streams _____

6. erosion_____

7. deforestation_____

8. noise pollution _____

At Home in the Biome

Gather students in groups of three. Give each person in the group a large piece of drawing paper labeled with one of the following biome names. Make sure all eight biomes are used on at least one of the pages. Provide crayons, pens, and markers. Give students these directions.Wait a few minutes between the steps to allow them time to draw.

1. Read the name of the biome at the top of the paper.

2. Draw the background to show the basic location or setting of the biome.

3. Pass your paper to the person on your right.

4. Draw plants that would be found in the biome background that your neighbor gave you.

5. Pass your paper again to the right.

6. This time, draw animals that would be found in the biome.

Biomes:	tropical rain forest	grassland	taiga
	fresh water	salt water	temperate deciduous forest
	tundra	desert	

Name that Phylum!

Find the name for the phylum that matches each description or group of animals:

_____ 1. have a central cavity and a mouth, most have tentacles

_____ 2. frog, shark, alligator, eagle, gorilla

_____ 3. tube-shaped body divided into segments, bristles that help movement

_____ 4. jellyfish, hydra, sea anemone, coral

_____ 5. snail, slug, squid, octopus, oyster

_____ 6. starfish, sea cucumber, sea urchin

_____ 7. each organism a thick sack of cells that form pores, chambers, or canals

_____ 8. jointed limbs, hard plated body covering, segmented bodies

Baffling Behaviors

Animals have such interesting behaviors. Write the names of these behaviors on the board or on a poster. Read the descriptions. Match the behaviors to the correct description.

1. Canada geese move to a warmer place for the winter.

2. A cat grows thicker fur in the winter

3. A male pigeon struts and bows in front of a female.

4. A brown bird turns white when snow collects on the ground.

5. A bear eats a lot of food, gets fat, and goes to sleep for a long time.

6. A lizard's tail gets broken off, so he grows a new tail!

7. An angler fish looks just like the rocks on the ocean floor.

8. A goose hisses when another animal comes near his home area.

9. A spider spins a web, even though nobody taught her how.

10. Wolves hunt and live in packs.

Such behavior!
regeneration
migration
instinct
courtship
camouflage
social behavior
mimicry
territoriality
adaptation
hibernation

Could It Be?

Use this oral quiz to review classification of animals. Answer each question *yes* or *no*. Explain the answer. (Tell why it could be or why it could NOT be.)

1. An animal has two pair of antennae. Could it be an insect?

2. An animal has a two-chambered heart and cold blood. Could it be a bird?

3. An animal lives in water and breathes with gills. Could it be a fish?

4. An animal has claw-like legs and sharp jaws. Could it be a crustacean?

5. An animal has four pairs of legs. Could it be a centipede?

6. An animal has two pairs of legs on each body segment. Could it be a millipede?

7. An animal has a three-chambered heart and smooth skin. Could it be an amphibian?

8. An animal has a four-chambered heart and warm blood. Could it be a reptile?

Busy Systems

Every human body system is made up of organs that work together to perform a function.

1. Describe the function of each of the systems below.

2. Name three or more organs that have a particular job in the system. Try to name several organs for each system. Try to name organs that you may not have known about before.

3. See if you can name five or more organs that work in more than one system.

Systems:

Respiratory

Endocrine

Skeletal

Waste Removal

Sensory-Nervous

Reproductive

Muscular

Circulatory

Integumentary

Digestive

Jobs Around the Body

Every part of the human body has a job to do. Do you know what the jobs are? Write a job description for as many of these body parts as you can in the time you have.

1. larynx

2. epiglottis

3. gallbladder

4. neurons

5. joints

6. bladder

7. diaphragm

8. kidneys

9. bronchi

10. liver

11. lungs

12. skin

13. ligaments

14. pituitary gland

15. salivary gland

16. arteries

17. pancreas

18. tongue

19. cartilage

20. spinal cord

Bone Maps

Pair students to strengthen knowledge of the major bones in the human body. Use self-adhesive note pads to label the "bone maps."

1. Write the names of the major bones, each one on a self-adhesive note:

humerus	metacarpals	phalanges	pelvis
tibia	patella	carpals	scapula
radius	ribs	skull	metatarsals
ulna	tarsals	mandible	femur
fibula	clavicle	sternum	

2. Turn your body (or a friend's body) into a bone map by sticking the notes to the correct places.

3. Finish a bone map for both partners in ten minutes.

Follow that Cell

Read these descriptions of where a blood cell is on its journey around the circulatory system. After students hear each description, they should name the location.

1. I'm in the largest vein in the body. Where am I?

2. I'm in an opening between the left atrium and the left ventricle. Where am I?

3. I've just entered the heart. Where am I?

4. I'm in a vessel that supplies blood to the brain. Where am I?

5. I'm full of oxygen, headed from the lungs toward the heart. Where am I?

6. I've just left the heart after exiting the left ventricle. Where am I?

7. I've just exchanged carbon dioxide for oxygen. Where am I?

8. I'm in one of the tiniest blood vessels in the body. Where am I?

Trick Your Brain

Use three bowls of water to challenge your students' senses and their brains.
Try this easy experiment, and then explain the mixed-up messages!

1. Fill one bowl ½ full of hot water.

2. Fill one bowl ½ full of cold water.

3. Fill one bowl ½ full of room temperature water.

4. Place the bowls on a table with the hot water by your left hand, the cold water by your right hand, and the room temperature water in the middle.

5. Set a timer for three minutes.

6. Put your left hand in the hot water and your right hand in the cold water.

7. When the timer rings, take both hands out and shake them off. Put both hands immediately into the center bowl.

8. Tell how the water feels to your right hand. Tell how the water feels to your left hand.

What's Happening?

The room temperature water feels different to both hands because the messages sent from the hands' sensory receptors to the brain are confused. The right hand adapted to the cold water, so the center bowl's water feels hot. The left hand adapted to the hot water, so the center bowl's water feels cold.

Call the Doctor!

Read the patient's complaints. Allow students to decide what the doctor's diagnosis might be. Name the disease or disorder.

1. Doctor, doctor, my bronchioles are blocked and I'm struggling for air.

2. Doctor, doctor, my appendix is inflamed.

3. Doctor, doctor, my joints are swollen all the time.

4. Doctor, doctor, a blood clot is blocking the artery to my brain.

5. Doctor, doctor, I have a serious liver infection.

6. Doctor, doctor, my voice box is inflamed.

7. Doctor, doctor, my gums are infected.

8. Doctor, doctor, I have a serious viral infection of my spinal nerves.

9. Doctor, doctor, I have an infection of the stomach and intestines.

10. Doctor, doctor, my parotid glands are infected.

First Aid Quiz

Someone has recommended first aid actions for the following emergencies. Assign one emergency to a pair of students who work to find out if the recommendation is a good one. Allow time for each pair to report their findings to the group.

1. Ailment: **bleeding**   Recommendation: *Put pressure on the wound with a clean cloth.*

2. Ailment: **insect sting**   Recommendation: *Do not remove the stinger.*

3. Ailment: **fainting**   Recommendation: *Lay victim flat on ground with feet up.*

4. Ailment: **snakebite**   Recommendation: *Keep victim moving around.*

5. Ailment: **minor burn**   Recommendation: *Pour warm water on the burn.*

6. Ailment: **frostbite**   Recommendation: *Soak frostbitten part in warm water.*

7. Ailment: **poisoning**   Recommendation: *Call a poison control center.*

8. Ailment: **nosebleed**   Recommendation: *Pinch nostrils together. Sit quietly, lean forward.*

9. Ailment: **hypothermia**   Recommendation: *Get victim into warm, dry clothes.*

10. Ailment: **heat exhaustion**   Recommendation: *Keep the victim warm.*

11. Ailment: **splinter**   Recommendation: *Dig the splinter out with a needle right away.*

12. Ailment: **shock**   Recommendation: *Keep the victim standing.*

Would You? Could You?

Carefully consider these fitness and nutrition questions. Answer each one *yes* or *no*.

1. Could you find protein in lentils? _____

2. Could you get aerobic benefit from stretching? _____

3. Could you increase flexibility with weightlifting? _____

4. Could you get carbohydrates from a bowl of peaches? _____

5. Could you get a good supply of fat from cheese or butter? _____

6. Would you help your body repair damaged cells if you ate fish? _____

7. Would you be building heart strength if you went biking regularly? _____

8. Would you get fiber in your diet by eating yogurt? _____

9. Would you build strength if you paddled a canoe regularly? _____

10. Would you build arm strength by climbing stairs? _____

A Guide to the Tongue

Lead students in this investigation in small groups to teach the way around the tongue.

1. Gather these supplies: four small glasses half full of water, cotton swaps, tissue, salt, sugar, an aspirin tablet, and vinegar.

2. Make a solution of salt and water (salty), a solution of sugar and water (sweet), a solution of aspirin dissolved in water (bitter), and a solution with a tablespoon of vinegar and water (sour).

3. Draw four tongue shapes on a piece of paper. Label them salty, sweet, bitter, and sour.

4. Dip a cotton swab in the salt water. Tap it on the side of the glass to get rid of excess liquid.

5. Wipe your tongue with tissue.

6. Touch the swab to the tip, sides, middle, and back of your tongue. Pay attention to the strength of the taste in each location. Color the area of the "salty" tongue map where the salty taste is strongest.

7. Repeat this process with a new swab for each of the other three tastes.

Gene Check

Take a survey of all the students in your class or grade. Count the number of people who show each of these gene-determined traits.

_____ blue eyes

_____ brown eyes

_____ blonde hair

_____ brown hair

_____ red hair

_____ curly hair

_____ straight hair

_____ dimples

_____ freckles

_____ can wiggle little toe

_____ can touch tongue to the tip of nose

_____ can bend fingers at the top joint

_____ can curl tongue

_____ can spread toes apart

_____ can spread index and middle finger from little finger and ring finger

What's the Difference? (I)

Students often confuse these events, items, or ideas with one another in the study of life science. Make sure they can explain the difference. Split the list among a few groups. Each group should track down a clear explanation for each word in a pair, so the difference is evident.

1. osmosis and plasmolysis

2. xylem and phloem

3. pollination and fertilization

4. cornea and iris

5. hibernation and migration

6. producer and consumer

7. predator and parasite

8. epithelial tissue and connective tissue

9. cerebrum and cerebellum

10. tibia and fibula

11. identical twins and fraternal twins

12. complete metamorphosis and incomplete metamorphosis

Where Would You Find It? (III)

Look at each word. Find out about the earth and space science feature that the word names. Describe a place where this item or condition would be found.

1. corona

2. convection zone

3. atoll

4. archipelago

5. coma

6. typhoon

7. umbra

8. asteroid belt

9. magma

10. mantle

11. millwater

12. aquifer

13. abyssal plain

14. sirocco

15. wormhole

16. nebulae

17. mudpot

18. lagoon

Extraterrestrial Questions

Thousands of interesting items other than the major planets are whirling around beyond Earth. Check up on extraterrestrial awareness by posing these questions aloud. Ask for a yes or no answer. If the answer is no, students should explain why.

1. Is cosmic dust likely to be found between planets?

2. Is a comet's coma thicker than its nucleus?

3. Is a comet named after the observatory used during its discovery?

4. Is the asteroid belt found between Mercury and Venus?

5. Is a fireball a name for an unusually bright asteroid?

6. Could a meteorite be seen flying through space?

7. Do comets orbit the Sun?

8. Is a meteor sometimes called a shooting star?

9. Could a comet's tail be as long as a million miles?

10. Is it true that part of a comet is frozen?

Sun Design

Match the Sun's major features with their correct descriptions. Post the following list where students can see it easily. Give a group of two or three students one of the descriptions below and a good reference book so they can match the correct name to the description.

1. element that makes up 70% of Sun's composition

2. visible surface of the Sun, emits radiation seen from Earth

3. sudden increases in brightness of the chromosphere

4. area where energy flows out in waves beyond the core

5. relatively cooler areas of the Sun that look dark

6. area where waves of energy churn around

7. surges of glowing gas rising from the Sun's surface

8. bright red layer of gas extending out from the photosphere

9. outer atmosphere of Sun visible from Earth only during an eclipse

10. low density stream of charged particles given off by the Sun

> core
> helium
> sunspots
> solar wind
> oxygen
> radioactive zone
> convection zone
> solar flares
> photosphere
> corona
> prominences
> chromosphere
> hydrogen

Planetary Trivia

Divide the class into small groups. Provide science reference books. Each group should find several facts about planets to use as clues in a game. They can write each clue on a separate card.

When facts are collected, create a game to play with the clues.

Sample Clues:

1. It has ice caps at both poles.

2. It is the 8th planet from Sun.

3. It is the largest planet.

4. The length of its day is similar to Earth's.

5. It is a blue-green planet.

6. It has 2 moons.

7. Its rotation takes about 10 hours.

8. It takes 165 Earth years to orbit the Sun.

9. It has the shortest year.

10. It is called "the red planet."

11. It has the most severely tilted axis.

12. It has retrograde rotation.

13. It has over 1,000 rings.

14. Its moons are named for Shakespearean characters.

15. It is known as the windy planet.

Moon Matters

Focus on matters of fact about Earth's moon. Read each statement. Decide if it is true. If it is not, restate it to make it true.

1. Earth's moon emits light through radiation.

2. The moon rotates once during its revolution.

3. The moon revolves around Earth once every 29.5 days

4. The moon has violent weather.

5. In the cycle of moon phases, a waxing gibbous follows the full moon.

6. A lunar eclipse occurs when Earth passes through the Moon's shadow.

7. During a solar eclipse, you should only look at the Sun through sunglasses.

8. In the shadow cast during an eclipse, the umbra is the part that is darker than the penumbra.

Calling All Stargazers

Use this oral activity to tune-up astronomy knowledge. Pretend students are stargazers visually "cruising" the universe. Ask students what they are looking at if they see each of these ten things.

1. clouds of dust and gas where stars are born

2. an object formed when a massive star collapses due to gravity

3. a star suddenly exploding with increasing brightness

4. the brightest star in the sky

5. the core of a star left after a supernova explosion

6. billions of stars held together by gravitational attraction

7. a white dwarf that has stopped radiating energy

8. a star whose brightness changes

9. most common type of star

10. pair of stars that orbit each other or appear to orbit each other

Lions, Scorpions, Dragons, & Crabs

Constellations are groups of stars that create shapes or patterns. Ancient stargazers gave names to eighty-eight different constellations. Here is a quick way to make replica of a constellation.

1. Get a piece of black paper. Cut an 8-inch (or 20-cm) square.

2. Use chalk to draw a 6-inch (10-cm) circle.

3. Choose a familiar constellation. Study its pattern. Pay attention to the different sizes of the stars in the constellation.

4. Use chalk to draw the constellation in the circle. Mark circles for the stars.

5. Use a needle, pin, or paper clip to poke holes for each star in the constellation. Poke larger holes for the larger stars.

6. Get a 3-pound coffee can or a large juice can. Remove both ends.

7. Use a rubber band to fasten the black paper over one end of the can.

8. Go to a dark room. Shine a flashlight through the bottom of the can so the light passes through the black paper. Project the constellation onto the ceiling.

News Flash!

Turn some of the great moments in space exploration into news headlines. Give one of these events (or others like it) and science reference books to a small group of two to three students. Ask them to turn their brief description of a space exploration event into a news headline. They should create the headline and an opening paragraph for the news report on that event.

1543 — Copernicus claimed that the Sun was at the center of the universe

1920s — Edwin Hubble demonstrated that the universe is expanding

1926 — launch of first liquid-propelled rocket

1957 — the launch of Sputnik I

1961 — first American launched into space

1969 — landing of first humans on moon

1981 — landing of first space shuttle (Columbia)

1990 — launch of Hubble Space Telescope

1998 — launch of first pieces of International Space Station

2001 — first space tourist launched

1930 — New Planet Discovered

Scientists celebrate as a ninth planet has been discovered. Some scientists think it is a wandering moon, but Pluto officially has been declared a planet.

Get it Right

Distribute maps and markers and get busy searching for some of the most prominent features on Earth's surface. If the maps are not laminated, cover them with plastic wrap. Using a marker, students should circle an example of each of these features.

Compile a list of the names and locations of each feature. Students might work in teams to challenge one another in this search.

Find a(n) . . .

___ archipelago	___ desert	___ cape
___ fjord	___ channel	___ delta
___ peak	___ strait	___ island
___ volcano	___ canyon	___ isthmus
___ gulf	___ bay	___ sea
___ peninsula	___ lake	___ plain

Do-It-Yourself Volcano

After you review the details about what a volcano is and how it develops, make a volcano replica to mimic the action of the real thing.

1. Put some liquid soap, red food coloring, and a few spoonfuls of baking soda in a plastic soda bottle.

2. Start with a base of wood or heavy cardboard.

3. Get a supply of modeling clay, play dough, plaster, or dirt to form a mountain.

4. Build the mountain around the bottle.

5. When the mountain is finished, quickly and carefully pour some vinegar into the bottle opening.

6. Stand back and watch the action!

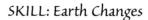

Changes Fast & Slow

See how many of these Earth surface changes (or products of Earth changes) students can describe or define in ten minutes. For each one, ask if the change is a fast or a slow one.

1) deflation
2) abrasion
3) weathering
4) delta
5) stalagmite
6) flood plain
7) landslide
8) mudslide

9) decomposition
10) mudflow
11) till
12) stalactite
13) dunes
14) creep
15) sinkhole
16) rock fall

17) cave
18) abrading
19) plucking
20) levee
21) fumarole
22) iceberg
23) disintegration
24) loess

Water-Wise

Try this quick "either-or" quiz to refresh yourself about some of the features of facts about groundwater, rivers, and oceans. Choose the correct answer from the two options.

1. Which is rolled along the bottom of a river: bed load OR suspended load?

2. Which makes its way through a delta: an estuary OR a tributary?

3. Which might smell most like sulfur: a geyser OR a fumarole?

4. Which deposit rises up from a cave floor: a stalagmite OR a stalactite?

5. Which is a funnel-shaped depression caused by dissolved limestone: a mudpot OR a sinkhole?

6. Which is closer to the shore: a continental shelf OR a continental slope?

7. Which can be seen above the surface of the water: a seamount OR an atoll?

8. An aquifer is made of which kind of rock: permeable OR impermeable?

9. Where would a spit build up: along a curved shoreline OR along a straight shoreline?

10. Which current is caused by differences in water temperature and chemical content: deep-water current OR a surface current?

Crests, Troughs, and Surf

How much do you know about waves? Listen carefully and follow the directions to show your understanding of wave features. Students will need drawing paper and pens, crayons, or markers.

Read the directions, allowing time for students to complete each step as you go.

1. Draw a series of waves coming up to a shoreline. Be sure to show the wave "tops" as well as the underwater ocean or lake bottom.

2. Draw a stick figure on a surfboard on the crest of one wave. Label the surfer **A**.

3. Draw a stick figure diver in a trough of a wave. Label the diver **B**.

4. Draw a line that shows the wavelength. Label this **C**.

5. Draw a line that shows the wave height. Label this **D**.

6. Draw a swimmer in the surf. Label the swimmer **E**.

7. Challenge: Find a shallow-water wave in your diagram. Label it **F**.

8. Challenge: Find a deep-water wave in your diagram. Label it **G**.

The Air Around Us

The atmosphere is the blanket of air that surrounds the Earth. Atmospheric pressure is the force of air pressing down on Earth's surface. Air pressure (or atmospheric pressure) varies at different places. It is affected by temperature and altitude.

Do this short experiment to get a close-up look at what air pressure does. Make sure you are near a sink or pan to catch spilling water. Watch the results of the experiment. As a class, discuss what happened.

1. Get an empty plastic soda bottle with a screw-on top.

2. Use scissors to poke a small hole on the side of the bottle near the bottom.

3. Fill the bottle to the very top (no space left over) with water. Hold your finger over the hole so no water drains out of the bottle.

4. Keep holding your finger over the hole while you screw the top on tightly.

5. Take your finger away from the hole. (Be careful not to squeeze the bottle.)

6. Describe what happens. Ask students to explain the results.

Wind Watch

Name the Wind!

1. They blow toward the equator from 30°N latitude or 30°S latitude.

2. It is a hurricane in the northwestern Pacific Ocean.

3. They are cold, dry, dense horizontal air currents blowing from northeast to southwest between the North Pole and 60°N latitude in the northern hemisphere. In the southern hemisphere, they blow from southeast to northwest between the South Pole and 60°S latitude.

4. These are the prevailing winds in the middle latitudes. They blow from west to east.

5. This is a condition of no wind found along the equator.

6. These are strong winds that bring heavy rain to northern Australia and southern Asia.

7. It is a warm, dry wind that flows down the side of a mountain range.

8. They are narrow belts of fast-moving air flowing in a westerly direction in the higher levels of the troposphere.

Weather or Not?

Give a weather condition from the list to a pair of students. Their job is to find the specific details and definition of that condition and create a weather report that forecasts it—or not. Their forecast can be accurate or phony. When the reports are presented to the class, classmates must decide whether the report is accurate. They show their decision by raising a sign that says "Weather" if the description is correct OR a sign that says "NOT!" if the description is in error.

Examples:

Frozen raindrops will keep refreezing and fall to the ground as heavy dew.

"NOT!"

We are officially in a drought period. There has been no precipitation for weeks.

"Weather!"

Weather Conditions

snow	blizzard
hail	rain
sleet	thunderstorm
drought	hurricane
cyclone	tornado
dew	monsoon
typhoon	high humidity
cold front	tornado watch
warm front	

What's the Difference? (II)

These are events, items, or ideas that students often get confused with one another in the study of earth and space science. Make sure you can explain the difference. Split the list among a few groups. Instruct the groups to track down a clear explanation for each word in a pair, so the difference is made evident.

1. isthmus and strait

2. galaxy and universe

3. magma and lava

4. rock and mineral

5. topsoil and loess

6. fold and fault

7. biosphere and atmosphere

8. solar eclipse and lunar eclipse

9. dormant volcano and extinct volcano

10. star luminosity and star magnitude

11. Earth's mantle and Earth's crust

12. renewable resource and nonrenewable resource

Where Would You Find It? (IV)

Look at each word. Find out about the feature from the physical sciences that the word names. Describe a place where this item or condition would be found.

1. proton

2. neutron

3. atomic number

4. nucleus

5. crest

6. pole

7. electron

8. catalyst

9. chemical bonds

10. gamma ray

11. a solute

12. inertia

13. magnetic field

14. names of elements

15. radiant energy

16. potential energy

17. electric current

18. microwaves

Ten Words or Less

Matter is the material that makes up all things in the universe. Each substance has properties. Give students a chance to review the properties of matter. Divide students into small groups of two or three. Provide each group with the following list. They must use ten minutes to create a definition or explanation of each, using ten words or less.

1. weight

2. density

3. freezing point

4. boiling point

5. magnetism

6. mass

7. volume

8. corrosion

9. viscosity

10. physical property

11. chemical property

12. hardness

An Icy Trick

Lift an ice cube out of water just by touching it with a string. No knots or loops are needed around the ice cube. Collect these supplies: ice cubes, a glass of water, a 2-foot (60-cm) piece of string, and salt. To do the experiment with a group, collect enough supplies to allow students to work in several small groups.

1. Gently set an ice cube on top of the water in the glass.

2. Wet the string and lay it across the top of the ice cube.

3. Sprinkle salt over the string in the area where it touches the ice.

4. Wait for a few minutes.

5. Carefully pick up the ends of the string and lift the ice cube out of the water.

6. Record the results and try to explain how it works.

Spinning Eggs

Use eggs to examine one way density affects the behavior of matter.

1. Get a raw egg and a hard-boiled egg.

2. Mark a stripe on the hard-boiled egg so you can tell them apart.

3. Stand each egg on one end and spin it.

4. Record the results.

5. Next, spin each egg on its side.

6. Try to stop them both with one touch of your finger.

7. Record the results.

8. Try to explain the results.

Density is the amount of mass packed into a given unit. It is the ratio of an object's mass to its volume. As density increases, molecules of a substance are closer together, because there are more molecules per cubic unit.

The Sinking Egg

Explore the property of density by watching what happens when it changes Gather these supplies: a glass jar, water, salt, a measuring cup, a large spoon, and a raw egg.

1. Fill the jar half-full of water.

2. Gently place a raw egg in the water.

3. Record what happens.

4. Remove the egg carefully.

5. Stir ¼ cup of salt into the water.

6. Gently place the egg back into the water.

7. Make a record of what happens.

8. Explain the results of the experiment.

Density is the amount of mass packed into a given unit. It is the ratio of an object's mass to its volume. As density increases, molecules of a substance are closer together, because there are more molecules per cubic unit.

A Famous Table

Find the mystery elements to match the clues below. Work together in a small or large group to solve each mystery. Get help from this diagram and a copy of the Periodic Table.

1. has 22 electrons
2. is the symbol for tungsten
3. mass is 100 less than cerium
4. has 121 neutrons and 80 electrons
5. has 12 neutrons
6. has 42 neutrons

7. has mass of 204
8. has 79 electrons
9. has 6 neutrons and 6 electrons
10. has 7 neutrons
11. has mass of 91
12. has 29 protons

Remember:

atomic mass = number of protons + number of neutrons
atomic number = number of protons
number of protons = number of electrons

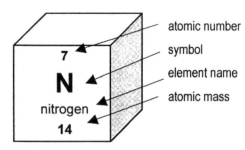

atomic number
symbol
element name
atomic mass

7
N
nitrogen
14

What's True About Mixtures?

Put your knowledge about mixtures to work to decide which of these statements are true. If a statement is not true, tell why.

1. Particles are spread evenly throughout a heterogeneous mixture.

2. Orange juice with pulp is an example of a homogeneous mixture.

3. The particles of a mixture can be filtered out.

4. Some mixtures can be separated out by distillation.

5. The particles in a colloid can be filtered out.

6. A suspension is a heterogeneous mixture.

7. Root beer is an example of a homogeneous mixture.

8. A milkshake is an example of a homogeneous mixture.

9. Salt water is a heterogeneous mixture.

10. A suspension looks clear.

What's True About Solutions?

Put your knowledge about solutions to work to decide which of these statements are true. If a statement is not true, tell why.

1. In a solution, two or more substances are mixed uniformly.

2. In a solution, the solvent is the substance being dissolved.

3. The concentration in a solution is the amount of solute dissolved per unit of solvent.

4. In a gaseous solution, gas is dissolved in a liquid.

5. An unsaturated solution is a solution that holds all the solute possible.

6. A supersaturated solution holds all the solution it normally can.

7. In salt water, the water is the solvent.

8. Solubility can be increased by raising the temperature of the solvent.

9. Water is the solvent in an aqueous solution.

10. In a solid solution, a solid is dissolved in a gas or liquid.

Clean Your Pennies

Use this solution to make old pennies look like new.

1. Gather these supplies: glass jar, measuring spoons, water, vinegar, salt, paper towels, and dirty pennies.

2. Mix 3 tablespoons of vinegar and 1 tablespoon of salt in the jar.

3. Drop the dirty pennies in the jar.

4. Wait a few minutes.

5. Remove the pennies, rinse, and dry them.

6. Do some research to find out why the pennies got clean.

   A solution is a homogeneous mixture in which one substance (a solute) is dissolved in another (a solvent).

What Kind of Change?

In each of these events a change in matter is taking place. Is it a physical change or a chemical change? Read the events aloud, one at a time, while students label them **P** for physical change or **C** for chemical change.

_____ 1. spoiling food

_____ 2. a glass breaking

_____ 3. freezing popsicles

_____ 4. making salt water to gargle

_____ 5. burning leaves

_____ 6. a rusting bicycle

_____ 7. fireworks exploding

_____ 8. hammering wood to make a birdhouse

_____ 9. evaporating water

_____ 10. melting butter

_____ 11. glassblower blowing glass

_____ 12. whipping cream

_____ 13. bleaching hair

_____ 14. burning toast

_____ 15. squeezing lemons to make lemonade

_____ 16. frying an egg

Common Combinations

A compound is a combination of one or more elements. The elements have been chemically combined—meaning that the nature of each individual substance is changed to produce a new substance. Read the names of these everyday compounds. Use science references to find the chemical formula for as many as possible in ten minutes.

1. marble

2. bleach

3. table salt

4. baking soda

5. sand

6. hydrogen peroxide

7. lime

8. milk of magnesia

9. sugar

10. candle wax

11. Freon

12. ammonia

The Great Paper Race

Use this simple experiment to spark a discussion about air pressure, gravity, and resistance. Repeat the experiment several times to draw conclusions about the results.

1. Start with two identical pieces of drawing paper or typing paper.

2. Leave one piece flat, and crumple the other piece into a ball.

3. Stand on a table, chair, or ladder to increase your distance from the ground.

4. Drop both pieces of paper at the same time.

5. Instruct students to watch carefully to see how quickly each paper reaches the ground.

6. If you wish, use stopwatches to time each paper.

7. Discuss and explain the results.

Define It!

Sometimes the different concepts and terms related to force and energy get confusing. Straighten out the confusion by offering concrete examples for each idea.

Give one of the following terms to each pair of students. Give them ten minutes to think of a real-life example that demonstrates the meaning and concept to others. Find a time for them to share the examples with the whole group.

> The **force** from your legs helps you climb a step.
>
> **Energy** from the sun warms the air.

1. gravity
2. centrifugal force
3. centripetal force
4. friction
5. inertia
6. momentum

7. resistance
8. action—reaction
9. kinetic energy
10. potential energy
11. mechanical energy
12. work

13. radiant energy
14. acceleration
15. velocity
16. deceleration

A Straw With Muscle

Gather a pile of raw, unpeeled potatoes. Then, collect enough drinking straws so that everyone in the group can show off their strength. (The straw shows off its strength, too.) All it takes is force and a little practice.

1. Hold a potato in one hand.

2. Hold a straw in the other hand, covering the top end with your index finger.

3. Hold the straw straight up (at a right angle to the potato) and plunge it into the potato.

4. Watch what happens.

5. Try to explain the results and discuss them as a class.

The Powerful Nickel

Line up some nickels to get a look at principles of motion. Divide students into groups, giving each group five nickels. Ask the groups to complete the experiment and discuss the results. Each group should try to explain what happened and why.

1. Line up four of the nickels on a smooth table top. Place the nickels so that they touch each other.

2. Line up the fifth nickel with the others, but do not let it touch them. Place it two inches back from the row of four nickels.

3. Snap your third finger against the loose coin, sending it sliding fast against the row of four nickels.

4. Watch what happens.

Catch a Falling Dollar

Learn a few things about force and motion with this experiment. All you need is a dollar bill a volunteer to try to catch it. It falls so quickly that everyone will have time to give it a try.

1. The volunteer rests her or his arm on a table with one open hand hanging over the edge of the table.

2. The volunteer should open her or his fingers from the thumb, in a position ready to catch the dollar.

3. Hold the dollar bill between the parted thumb and fingers, with half of the bill above the student's hand.

4. Let the volunteer know that the object is to grab the dollar bill (between fingers and thumb) when it falls.

5. Don't tell the volunteer when you are ready to let the dollar bill go. Just drop it.

6. Let each person in the group try this.

7. Discuss the results.

Which Law?

Review Newton's Laws of Motion with students. Display the laws where all students can see them. Read the examples below. Ask students to decide which law of motion is demonstrated by each "scenario."

Law # 1 (inertia): An object at rest remains at rest or an object in motion continues moving in a straight line at a steady rate until a force acts on it.

Law # 2 (accelerated motion): The amount of force needed to change the speed of an object depends on the mass of the object and the amount of acceleration or deceleration needed.

Law # 3 (action—reaction pairs): For every action (force) there is an opposite and equal reaction (force).

1. As an ice skater pushes harder with her muscles, she begins to move faster.

2. A swimmer pushes water backward with his arms, but his body moves forward.

3. A frog leaps off a lily pad. He is pulled downward by gravity and lands on another lily pad instead of continuing the movement in a straight line.

4. A boy paddles the canoe by pulling back on the paddle. The canoe goes forward.

5. It takes more force to get a sled with two people on it moving than a sled with one person.

6. A girl speeds downhill on a sled. The sled hits a rock. The girl is thrown forward and keeps going downhill without the sled.

Leaping Popcorn

Collect these supplies to demonstrate the great powers of static electricity: a large bag of dry popcorn, several plates, scraps of wool cloth (or old wool hats, socks, or sweaters), and several rubber combs or old LP records. Divide students into small groups. Give each group a small bag of popcorn, a plate, a wool item, and a comb or record.

1. Spread the popcorn on the plate.

2. Rub the comb (or record) vigorously with the wool.

3. Hold the comb (or record) toward the popcorn.

4. Describe and explain what happens.

A Warm Warm-Up

Try to answer all ten questions about heat in ten minutes. The speed of your thinking should generate some heat!

1. How does heat get from the stove burner into your soup?

2. Why doesn't a plastic spoon in your hot chocolate feel hot to your hand?

3. Why is the attic of a house warmer than the basement?

4. When you turn on the heater in your car, how does the heat reach you?

5. Why does a metal spoon in your hot chocolate feel hot to your hand?

6. How does heat from the Sun reach your body?

7. Why does clean snow melt more slowly than dirty snow?

8. How can a solar heating system heat your house on a cloudy day?

9. Why is our hot water heater wrapped in a thick cover?

10. Why does ice melt in my soda?

The Amazing, Hearing Teeth

Did you know you can hear through your teeth? Get a supply of metal forks and metal spoons. Divide the group into pairs, giving each pair a spoon and a fork. Then try this trick to demonstrate how sound travels.

1. Bang the spoon against the fork to make the fork "ring."

2. Hold the fork until the sound begins to fade.

3. When you can't hear the ringing any more, put the handle of the fork between your front teeth.

4. Bite down firmly on the fork handle and listen.

5. Describe and explain what happens.

The Changing Pencil

Use the amazing properties of light for this trick. Watch a pencil grow shorter or longer or fatter—right before your eyes. Students can work in small groups to do this experiment. Each group needs a jar of water and two identical pencils of the same length.

1. Place one pencil in the center of the jar of water.

2. Hold the second pencil next to the outside edge of the jar so you can compare it with the pencil inside the jar.

3. Lower your head close to the jar and look straight down at the pencil in the water.

4. Describe what you see.

5. Hold your face close to the side of the jar and look at the pencil inside of it.

6. Describe what you see.

What's the Difference? (III)

Students often confuse these events, items, or ideas with one another in the study of physical science. Make sure they can explain the difference. Split the list among a few groups. Challenge the groups to track down a clear explanation for each word in a pair, so that the difference between them is evident.

1. mixture and solution

2. motion and force

3. speed and velocity

4. acid and base

5. element and compound

6. reflection and refraction

7. transparent and translucent

8. condensation and evaporation

9. direct current and indirect current

10. series circuit and parallel circuit

11. potential energy and kinetic energy

12. conductor and insulator

Answers

PAGE 9

Answers will vary.

PAGE 10

1. parts of organisms and their relationships to each other
2. life forms from prehistoric times
3. soil and crop-raising
4. matter and energy
5. blood
6. behavior of matter at very low temperatures
7. rocks
8. insects
9. structures of cells
10. birds
11. past human cultures
12. tissues
13. heredity and genes
14. diseases
15. physical processes in the working of objects in space
16. fish
17. animals
18. plants

PAGE 11

1) When a foreign substance gets inside an oyster, the cells inside the shell produce a substance called nacre and coat the foreign object in layers until the object is encased. The encased object is called a pearl.
2) Tides are at their highest and lowest during spring tides because the Earth, Moon, and Sun are lined up with each other, causing greater gravitational pulls than during neap tides, when the Sun and Moon are at right angles from each other.
3) The elephant is using its sense of smell, constantly sniffing the air for danger.
4) A black hole is a collapsed star with so much gravitational pull that anything near it is pulled inside and cannot escape.
5) the year 2062
6) A diamond is made of carbon, whose atoms are in a structure that is very tightly held together.
7) Vacuoles store food or water in cells.
8) Cats ingest fur from cleaning themselves. The hair is not digestible, so they cough it up.
9) Do not struggle. Use slow swimming movements. Float on top and roll to solid ground.
10) a protein substance called keratin

PAGE 12

Answers may vary.

1. in the human body, shoulder region
2. in the nervous system of a body
3. in a cave
4. in the universe (or a galaxy)
5. in the back of the throat
6. in the brain
7. in the ocean
8. SE Asia or northern Australia
9. following a comet—in space
10. on a one-celled organism
11. in an atom
12. in the sky
13. in a volcanic area
14. along the equator
15. along the edge of a receding glacier
16. in a green plant
17. in a plant cell
18. along a shoreline

PAGE 13

1. 30,000
2. 25,000
3. 1.7

Answers

4. 7000
5. 460
6. 3,000,000
7. 0.147
8. 25,500
9. 35
10. 24.5
11. 44
12. 160.9
13. 53
14. 9.144
15. 28,349.5
16. 9.465

PAGE 14

1. Formula for area of a rectangular prism is A = l x w x h) *Answer:* yes
2. Formula for perimeter is P = sum of all sides. *Answer:* 5 hours
3. Formula for volume of a cylinder is V = B x h (B is the area of the base or A = pi r2). *Answer:* yes
4. (Formula for the volume

of a sphere is V = 4/3 pi r3. *Answer:* yes.
5. Formula for the area of a trapezoid is A = 1/2 (b1 + b2) h. *Answer:* 3 cans of paint are needed, total cost $37.50.
6. Formula for volume of a cone is V = 1/3 pi r2h. *Answer:* yes

PAGE 15

1. The formula for mechanical advantage of a lever is MA = le (length of the effort arm)/lr (length of the resistance arm. *Answer:* 44
2. The unit of force is a Newton. The formula for effort force (Fe) is Fe = Fr (resistance force)/MA (mechanical advantage). *Answer:* 300N
3. The unit of power is watts (W). The formula for power is P = w/t (Power = work (which is Force x distance) divided

by time). *Answer:* 18,000 W
4. The specific heat of water is 4,190. This means that it takes 4,190 joules to raise the temperature of 1 kilogram of water 1 degree C (Celsius). The formula for change in thermal energy is Q (change in thermal energy) = T (change in temperature) x M (mass) x Cp (specific heat of substance), *Answer:* 419,000 J
5. Electrical power is measured in watts. The formula for calculating electrical power is P = V (voltage) x I (current). *Answer:* 1,800 W
6. The unit of work is a joule (J). The formula for work is W = F (force) x d (distance). *Answer:* 350 J.

PAGE 16

1. Earth and other planets

revolve around the Sun.
2. Observations of time and space are relative to the observer.
3. The universe formed as the result of a giant, violent explosion.
4. Infectious diseases are caused by microorganisms.
5. All species of plant and animal life developed gradually from a small number of common ancestors.
6. The Earth has an outer shell of rigid plates that move about on a layer of hot, flowing rock.
7. The electrical resistance of a substance disappears at very low temperatures.
8. Every action has an equal and opposite reaction.
9. The pressure of a fluid increases as its velocity decreases.

10. Units called genes, which occur in pairs, determine heredity characteristics.

11. The acceleration of an object depends upon its mass and the applied force.

12. All objects exert an attractive force on one another.

13. Pressure applied to a fluid in an enclosed container is transmitted with equal force throughout the container.

14. The loss of weight of an object in water is equal to the weight of the displaced water.

PAGE 17

Answers may vary somewhat.

1. cycle
2. form & function
3. equilibrium
4. change
5. constancy
6. force & motion
7. order
8. cause & effect
9. system
10. energy & matter

PAGE 18

Answers will vary.

PAGE 19

Answers will vary.

PAGE 20

1. fire
2. light bulb
3. geometry
4. rocket
5. maps
6. blood circulation
7. mapping of human genome
8. Pluto
9. CDs
10. moon walk

PAGE 21

1. F
2. M
3. I
4. J
5. C
6. H
7. L
8. D
9. K
10. E
11. B
12. G
13. A
14. N

PAGE 22

Answers may vary somewhat.

1. on a leaf
2. in a plant
3. on a leaf
4. in the eye
5. in an ear
6. in blood
7. in a cell
8. in the heart
9. in the blood
10. in a flower
11. on a dead organism
12. at the top of the trachea
13. in the eye
14. on a host
15. in the brain
16. at the end of the spinal column
17. in a plant
18. inside bones

PAGE 23

1. diffusion (or passing) of water through a membrane
2. from an area of greater concentration to an area of lesser concentration
3. the cell nucleus
4. plasmolysis
5. energy
6. made of cells, need food, need water, produce waste, grow, reproduce, and respond to their environment
7. cell wall or chloroplasts

Answers

8. water
9. active transport
10. metabolism

PAGE 24

1. anchor the plant, absorb water and nutrients from soil
2. has vessels that move water and nutrients around the plant
3. traps sunlight
4. protects the inner parts of the leaf
5. makes plant stems strong and thick, makes new xylem and phloem cells
6. give support to the plant
7. attaches the leaf to the plant stem
8. anchor plants, take in nutrients, spring up new plants
9. produces seeds
10. opens and closes to let air and water into or out of the leaf

11. stores food for the plant

PAGE 25

1. Change sugar to chlorophyll.
2. Change veins to stomata.
3. Change germination to respiration
4. Change carbon dioxide to oxygen, OR, change photosynthesis to respiration.
5. Change oxygen to carbon dioxide OR, change respiration to photosynthesis.
6. Change transpiration to respiration.
7. Change geotropism to phototropism.
8. Change photosynthesis to respiration.

PAGE 26

no answers

PAGE 27

1. predator—prey

2. scavenger
3. parasitism
4. commensalism
5. dominant species
6. decomposer
7. mutualism
8. food chain
9. community
10. consumers

PAGE 28

Answers will vary. These are some possibilities.

1. sulfur dioxide
2. polluting chemicals
3. burning of fossil fuels
4. fog or pollution
5. hot water from factories
6. lack of vegetation
7. saws
8. airplanes and other vehicles or machines

PAGE 29

Drawings will vary. Check to see that background, plants,

and animals drawn are appropriate to each biome.

PAGE 30

1. coelenterata
2. chordata
3. annelida
4. coelenterata
5. mollusca
6. echinodermata
7. porifera
8. arthropoda

PAGE 31

1. migration
2. adaptation
3. courtship
4. camouflage
5. hibernation
6. regeneration
7. mimicry
8. territoriality
9. instinct
10. social behavior

PAGE 32

1. no
2. no
3. yes
4. yes
5. no
6. yes
7. yes
8. no

PAGE 33

Answers will vary somewhat. Make sure the organs listed for a system DO play a role in the functioning of that system.

Respiratory—takes in oxygen, transfers oxygen to the blood to be used by the body, and removes carbon dioxide from the body

Skeletal—gives shape and strength to the body; protects internal organs

Muscular—gives shape and strength to the body; allows the body to move

Sensory-Nervous—controls body functions and carries messages to and from the brain; allows the body to see, hear, smell, touch, taste, and feel

Endocrine—controls many body processes with chemical substances called hormones

Integumentary—covers and protects the body

Waste Removal—removes undigested solid wastes, water, carbon dioxide, wastes filtered from the blood, and other toxic substances from the body

Reproductive—provides for creation of new organisms

Circulatory—carries food and oxygen to the body cells, removes wastes and carbon dioxide

Digestive—changes food into a form that is usable by the body; removes waste material

PAGE 34

1. helps produce sounds (voice)
2. keeps food from going into the trachea
3. produces bile
4. join together to make nerves to transmit messages
5. allow body to bend
6. stores urine
7. assists breathing
8. remove waste from blood
9. carry air into and out of lungs
10. cleans waste from blood, stores useful substances
11. supply blood with oxygen, remove carbon dioxide from blood
12. protects body, helps to regulate body temperature
13. hold bones together, allow bending at joints
14. produces growth hormones
15. produces saliva to help with digestion
16. carry blood away from the heart
17. produces insulin
18. moves food toward esophagus, helps form words
19. cushions joints
20. carry messages from the brain

PAGE 35

humerus—upper arm bone

tibia—larger lower leg bone

radius—lower inside arm bone

ulna—lower outside arm bone

fibula—smaller bone in lower leg

metacarpals—hand bones

patella—knee cap

ribs—small bones that encase the heart and lungs

tarsals—ankle bones

clavicle—collar bone

phalanges—finger or toe bones

Answers

carpals—wrist bones
skull—head bone
mandible—jawbone
sternum—breast bone
pelvis—hip bones
scapula—shoulder blade
metatarsals—foot bones
femur—upper leg bone

PAGE 36

1. superior vena cava
2. valve
3. right atrium
4. carotid
5. pulmonary vein
6. aorta
7. lung
8. capillary

PAGE 37

no answers

PAGE 38

1. asthma
2. appendicitis
3. arthritis
4. stroke
5. hepatitis
6. laryngitis
7. pyorrhea
8. spinal meningitis
9. gastroenteritis
10. mumps

PAGE 39

1. yes
2. no
3. yes
4. no
5. no
6. yes
7. yes
8. yes
9. yes
10. no
11. no
12. no

PAGE 40

1. yes
2. no
3. no
4. yes
5. yes
6. yes
7. yes
8. no
9. yes
10. no

PAGE 41

no answers

PAGE 42

no answers

PAGE 43

1. **osmosis**—the diffusion of water through a cell membrane;
plasmolysis—the shrinking of cytoplasm in cells due to water loss
2. **xylem**—tissue that supports the plant in its roots and stems and carries water and nutrients to stems and leaves;
phloem—plant tissues with tubes that transport food to plant parts
3. **pollination**—movement of pollen from the stamen to the pistil of a flower;
fertilization—the joining of nuclei from male and female reproductive cells
4. **cornea**—the thin transparent covering of the eye;
iris—the colored part of the eye, the muscle that opens and closes the pupil
5. **hibernation**—a period when an animal goes to sleep for days, weeks, or months;
migration—moving a long distance to reproduce, mate, protect young, or find food
6. **producer**—an organism that makes its own food;
consumer—an organism that eats producers or

other organisms for its food

7. **predator**—one who pursues and eats another animal for food; **parasite**—an organism that lives on another organism to gain its sustenance

8. **epithelial**—outer layer tissue; **connective**—tissue that surrounds organs

9. **cerebrum**—the front part of the brain; **cerebellum**—smaller brain area at the back of the head

10. **tibia**—largest lower leg bone; **fibula**—smaller leg bone

11. **identical**—twins developed from one fertilized egg; **fraternal**—twins developed from two separate fertilized eggs

12. **complete**—the newborn has little resemblance to the adult animal; **incomplete**—the newborn looks like a small adult but lacks some features of an adult

PAGE 44

Answers may vary somewhat.

1. around the Sun
2. around the Sun
3. in an ocean
4. in a lake or ocean
5. on a comet
6. in the northwest Pacific Ocean
7. in an eclipse or on the surface of the Earth or Moon
8. between Mars and Jupiter
9. beneath Earth's crust
10. below the crust of Earth
11. under a glacier
12. in rock bed below Earth surface
13. under the ocean
14. in the Sahara Desert

15. in deep space
16. in a galaxy
17. in a volcanic area, in the ground
18. in an ocean

PAGE 45

1. yes
2. yes
3. no; A comet is named after the person who discovered it.
4. no; The asteroid belt is found between Mars and Jupiter.
5. no; A fireball is a name for an unusually bright meteor.
6. no; A meteor becomes a meteorite when it collides with Earth's surface.
7. yes
8. yes
9. yes
10. yes

PAGE 46

1. hydrogen
2. photosphere
3. solar flares
4. radioactive zone
5. sunspots
6. convection zone
7. prominences
8. chromosphere
9. corona
10. solar wind

PAGE 47

1. Mars
2. Neptune
3. Jupiter
4. Mars
5. Earth
6. Mars
7. Jupiter or Saturn
8. Neptune
9. Mercury
10. Mars
11. Uranus

Answers

12. Venus or Uranus
13. Saturn
14. Uranus
15. Neptune

PAGE 48

1. NO. The moon gives off no light. It only reflects light from the Sun.
2. YES
3. YES
4. NO. The moon has no weather.
5. NO. A waxing gibbous precedes the full moon. A waning gibbous follows the full moon.
6. NO. A lunar eclipse occurs when the moon passes through Earth's shadow.
7. NO. You should NEVER look directly at the Sun during a solar eclipse—not through sunglasses or anything else.
8. YES

PAGE 49

1. nebulae
2. black hole
3. supernova
4. Sirius A
5. neutron star
6. galaxy
7. black dwarf
8. variable star
9. red dwarf
10. binary stars

PAGE 50

No answers necessary. Check constellations against science/reference book for accuracy.

PAGE 51

Answers will vary.

PAGE 52

Answers will vary.

PAGE 53

No answers necessary.

PAGE 54

1. **deflation**—wind removes loose material from surfaces and drops it somewhere else, slow
2. **abrasion**—particles in the wind scour and scrape other surfaces, slow
3. **weathering**—wearing down or changing of rocks at or near the surface, slow
4. **delta**—land formed by deposits at the mouth of a river, slow
5. **stalagmite**—calcium carbonate deposits that develop from the floor of a cave, slow
6. **flood plain**—area where flooding river leaves sediment, slow or fast
7. **landslide**—quick movement of large amounts of material downhill, fast
8. **mudslide**—large masses of mud flow downslope quickly, fast
9. **decomposition**—chemical weathering where minerals in rocks are dissolved by water or react with substances in the air, slow
10. **mudflow**—masses of dirt and debris mixed with water move quickly downslope, fast
11. **till**—load of rocks, boulders, sand, and other debris carried by a moving glacier, slow
12. **stalactite**—calcium carbonate deposits that hang like an icicle from the roof of a cave
13. **dunes**—mounds or ridges of sand heaped by wind, slow or fast
14. **creep**—a mass of material moves slowly downslope, slow
15. **sinkhole**—funnel-shaped depression caused when limestone

dissolves rock beneath the ground, causing the ground to give way, slow or fast

16. **rock fall**—large masses of rock fall downslope quickly, fast

17. **cave**—large openings left in rocks when limestone in rocks dissolves, slow

18. **abrading**—scouring of rock surface by a moving glacier, slow

19. **plucking**—fragments picked up by a moving glacier and moved along, slow

20. **levee**—load of debris dropped at the edges of a riverbed by a flooding river, slow

21. **fumarole**—vents in the ground which give off steam and volcanic gasses, caused by volcanic activity, slow

22. **iceberg**—large blocks of ice that break from a glacier to float in the sea, slow

23. **disintegration**—physical weathering that breaks rocks down into smaller particles, slow

24. **loess**—fine dust that is deposited by wind, fast

PAGE 55

1. bed load
2. estuary
3. fumarole
4. stalagmite
5. sinkhole
6. continental shelf
7. atoll
8. permeable
9. curved shoreline
10. deep-water

PAGE 56

Check diagrams for accurate location of the following:

A. The wave crest is the highest point of a wave.

B. The wave trough is the lowest point of a wave.

C. The wavelength is the horizontal distance between two successive wave crests.

D. The wave height is the vertical distance from a wave's crest to the trough.

E. Surf is the area of breaking waves along the shore.

F. A shallow-water wave is a wave in water shallower than one-half its wavelength.

G. A deep-water wave is a wave in water deeper than one-half its wavelength.

PAGE 57

How It Works: When you filled the bottle, you left no room for air. There is no air to exert pressure on the water, so the water won't flow out. If you remove the bottle top, air pressure will push the water out through the hole in the bottle.

PAGE 58

1. trade winds
2. typhoon
3. polar easterlies
4. westerlies
5. doldrums
6. monsoons
7. chinook
8. jet streams

PAGE 59

Answers will vary

PAGE 60

1. **isthmus**—narrow strip of land joining two larger pieces of land; **strait**—narrow body of water joining two larger bodies of water

2. **galaxy**—large grouping of stars, planets, and other space objects; **universe**—the total of everything in outer space

Answers

3. **magma**—hot, molten rock beneath Earth's surface; **lava**—magma that has come to and spilled over Earth surface

4. **rock**—a combination of minerals; **mineral**—a substance made from only one kind of element

5. **topsoil**—the highest level of soil; **loess**—soil that has been blown around and deposited by the wind

6. **fold**—bend in rock; **fault**—a break in rock

7. **biosphere**—the layer around Earth where plants and animals live; **atmosphere**—the layer of air surrounding Earth

8. **solar eclipse**—Moon's shadow falling on Earth obscures all or part of the view of the Sun from Earth; **lunar eclipse**—the Moon passes through Earth's shadow, obscuring all or part of the view of the Moon from Earth

9. **dormant**—silent, inactive volcano; **extinct**—a volcano that has not had any activity for a very long time and probably won't again

10. **luminosity**—rate at which a star pours out energy; **magnitude (or brilliance)**—the brightness of a star as seen from Earth

11. **mantle**—the layer of Earth below the crust; **crust**—the outer layer of Earth

12. **renewable resource**—one that can be replaced by nature; **nonrenewable resource**—one that cannot be replaced by nature

PAGE 61
Answers may vary somewhat.
1. in the nucleus of an atom
2. in the nucleus of an atom
3. on a Periodic Table
4. in an atom
5. on a wave
6. on a magnet (or Earth)
7. in an atom
8. in a chemical reaction
9. in a chemical compound
10. on the electromagnetic spectrum
11. in a solution
12. in an object that is moving or at rest
13. near the end of a magnet
14. on a Periodic Table
15. anywhere touched by the Sun's rays
16. in a resting object
17. in a conductor
18. on the electromagnetic spectrum

PAGE 62
Answers will vary.
Possible answers:
1. force of gravity pulling on an object
2. amount of mass in a particular unit of mass (OR, mass of the material divided by its volume)
3. temperature at which the liquid form becomes solid
4. temperature at which the liquid form turns to gas
5. property of attracting certain other substances
6. amount of matter in an object
7. amount of space taken up by an object
8. ability to rust
9. describes how a substance pours
10. characteristic that can be observed
11. characteristics that describes how one substance will react with another
12. ability to scratch another substance

PAGE 63

How It Works: The salt causes the ice to melt along the string. Then the melted water refreezes into ice, freezing the wet string to the ice.

PAGE 64

How It Works: In the raw egg, the density varies. The egg yolk has a different density from the egg white, so the egg will not spin evenly. The density in a hard-boiled egg is the same throughout the egg, so the egg spins without wobbling.

PAGE 65

How It Works: The egg sinks in plain water because the water is not dense enough to hold up the egg. Adding salt makes the water more dense. This means the molecules are closer together and can keep the egg from sinking.

PAGE 66

1. titanium

2. W
3. calcium
4. mercury
5. sodium or magnesium
6. arsenic
7. thallium
8. gold
9. carbon
10. nitrogen
11. zirconium
12. copper

PAGE 67

1. NOT TRUE; particles are spread unevenly
2. NOT TRUE; orange juice with pulp is a suspension.
3. TRUE
4. TRUE
5. NOT TRUE; Particles in a colloid cannot be filtered out.
6. TRUE
7. TRUE
8. NOT TRUE; A milkshake is a heterogeneous mixture.
9. NOT TRUE; Salt water is a solution.
10. NOT TRUE; A suspension looks cloudy.

PAGE 68

1. TRUE
2. NOT TRUE; The solute is the substance being dissolved.
3. TRUE
4. NOT TRUE; In a gaseous solution, another substance is dissolved in a gas.
5. NOT TRUE; An unsaturated solution can hold more solute.
6. NOT TRUE; A supersaturated solution holds more solute than normal.
7. TRUE
8. TRUE
9. TRUE
10. NOT TRUE; In a solid solution, a solid, liquid, or gas is dissolved in a solid.

PAGE 69

How It Works: The vinegar (acetic acid) combined with the salt (sodium chloride) to make a new substance called hydrochloric acid. The hydrochloric acid is able to clean the pennies.

PAGE 70

1. C
2. P
3. P
4. P
5. C
6. C
7. C
8. P
9. P
10. P
11. P
12. P
13. C
14. C
15. P
16. C

Answers

PAGE 71

1. $CaCO_3$
2. $NaClO$
3. $NaCl$
4. CH_4
5. SiO_2
6. $H2O_2$
7. CaO
8. $Mg(OH)_2$
9. $C_{12}H_{22}O_{11}$
10. CH_2
11. CF_2C_{l2}
12. NH_3

PAGE 72

How It Works: The papers are the same size and shape. The crumpled paper takes up less space, so it has less surface area for the air to push against. This reduces the air resistance and allows the paper to fall faster.

PAGE 73

Answers will vary. Check to see that the example accurately portrays the concept.

PAGE 74

How It Works: Holding your finger over the end of the straw traps the air inside of it. When you drive the straw toward the potato, the air cannot be forced out of the straw. This air in the straw pushes out on the sides, keeping it so strong and solid that it will not collapse when you try to force it into the potato. The strength of the straw, combined with the force of your motion, allows the straw to poke a hole in the potato.

PAGE 75

What Happened? The nickels were at rest and remained so until a force acted on them. (This is the principle of inertia.) When the moving nickel hit the first nickel in the row, it stopped. The force of the moving nickel was transferred through the row of coins until it reached the last coin in the row. There was nothing to stop the last nickel, so the force caused it to move forward.

PAGE 76

What Happened? The force (gravity) causes objects to accelerate as they fall. (This means that they move faster and faster.) The dollar bill falls so fast that the brain can't receive the message and send it back to the fingers fast enough for the person to grab it. It is unlikely that anyone in your group will be able to catch it.

PAGE 77

1. # 2
2. # 3
3. # 1
4. # 3
5. # 2
6. # 1

PAGE 78

What Happened? When the comb (or record) is rubbed with wool, it picks up an electrical charge. The electrons in the "charged" comb (or record) attract the popcorn—which leaps to the comb. Once some of the electrons from the comb rub off on the popcorn, the popcorn gets a charge. Electrons have a negative charge. So the electrons in the popcorn push away from the electrons on the comb, and the popcorn leaps off the comb.

PAGE 79

1. by conduction
2. Plastic is a poor conductor of heat.
3. Cool air is more dense and heavier than warm air. It sinks and pushes warmer air upward.
4. by convection
5. Many metals are good conductors of heat.
6. by radiation

7. Clean snow reflects away some of the Sun's heat. Dirty snow, being darker, absorbs more radiant energy from the Sun.

8. The system has stored energy captured from the Sun on sunny days.

9. The cover is made of an insulating material—a material that does not carry heat well.

10. The heat from the warmer soda transfers to the ice cubes and melts them.

PAGE 80

What Happened? Solids such as your teeth and the bones in your ears are better conductors of sound than air is. Sound is caused by the vibrations of the fork. Placing the fork against your teeth allows the teeth to carry the vibrations through your head to the bones in your ears. You will be able to hear the ringing inside your head.

PAGE 81

What Happened? When light travels between two substances, its rays become bent. The light traveling from the air to the glass and the water bend. This bending light causes an object to look smaller or larger, depending on the angle of viewing.

PAGE 82

1. **mixture**—a combination of substances where the particles mix but there is no solution; **solution**—a combination of substances where one is dissolved in the other

2. **motion**—a change in position of matter; **force**—a push or pull on something

3. **speed**—the rate of motion; **velocity**—the rate of motion in a particular direction

4. **acid**—a chemical substance that reacts with metals to release hydrogen and produces hydronium ions when dissolved in water; **base**—a chemical substance that increases hydroxide ions when added to water

5. **element**—a substance made from only one kind of atom; **compound**—a substance made up of more than one element

6. **reflection**—the bouncing back of light off an object; **refraction**—the bending of light rays

7. **transparent**—able to be seen through; **translucent**—a substance that light passes through but is unable to be seen through

8. **condensation**—the change of a substance from a gas to a liquid; **evaporation**—the change of a substance from a liquid to a gas

9. **direct current**—electricity flowing in one direction; **indirect current**—electricity changing direction as it flows

10. **series circuit**—has only one path for electric current to follow; **parallel circuit** has two or more separate branches with different paths for the current to follow

11. **potential energy**——energy stored in an object at rest; **kinetic energy**—energy of motion

12. **conductor**—a substance through which electricity flows easily; **insulator**—a substance that resists or slows the flow of electricity